Skinfolk

AN AMERICAN SHOW

by Jillian Walker

53rd State Press
Brooklyn, NY

53 SP 44
September 2023
Brooklyn, NY

SKiNFOLK: An American Show
© Jillian Walker 2023
Scores © Jillian Walker & Kasaun Henry 2019
53rdstatepress.org

ISBN Number: 978-1732545274
Library of Congress Number: 2022931136

Book design: Jillian Walker + Kate Kremer
Cover design: w/d; cover image sourced from Das Pflanzensoziologische Institut (The Plant Sociological Institute), a non-profit association for the promotion of root research and its uses.

Printed on recycled paper in the United States of America.

SKiNFOLK: An American Show is made possible by the New York State Council on the Arts with the support of the Office of the Governor and the New York State Legislature.

AN AMERICAN SHOW

by Jillian Walker

with essays by Nia Witherspoon & Phillip Howze
53rd State Press | Brooklyn, NY

And if I am made a fool, it doesn't matter. No expression of love, Pure Love, ever hurt anybody.

– For my ancestors, seen and heard, unseen and unheard

INTRODUCTION

This is a sister-ritual-spell-play from a sister.
My sister, soon to be your sister (in some kind of way)
Or maybe your sis-tah.

It's an invitation for sure.
An invitation to dance (with spirits hers and yours)
Of course the invitation was written by you
when you (thought you) decided
but were guided to come on over
and stay a while ...

(...because there's a tiny
lasting shining part of you
that still remembers how to fly)

It's a wayward map
A map backwards through time
Asking us to face
them and theirs, ours and yours
(even back to the trees, first light/life)

And claim them.
Alllllladem.

It's a map downwards to the root and soil
That pulls no punches
And asks big questions like
What lies beneath the bottom of the family tree
...and
If we are truly family (like Sly said), what does that really mean?
...and
Can Blackness outrun the shame that birthed it?

It's a map unmade by Black.
Which is to say, a map unmade by faith.
Numbers unmade by story.
Percentages unmade by politics.
Black holds all, and has no need to be subdivided into parts that try pathetically to detract from its glory ("Bless her honor.")

A Black map.

A Black womanist mapping.
A naming. A litany. A lineage rite.
Not quite Kennedy's Duchess of Hapsburg, Queen Elizabeth, and Jesus
(though this is a Funnyhouse)
But Whitney. Prince. Black Pegasus. Ella, and Elegba
(the reference points of a decolonial Black mythos)

It's a calling.
To and From.
Is it yours?
Do you claim it?

○

"I dwell in possibility," croons Jillian Walker on a recent Instagram post. It is the sunset of winter. The cold still shakes our bones. The greedy and the needy conspire to wish away a pandemic that just won't quit, while we find ways to gather again inside the fiction of safety.

Some of us keep praying, wondering silently and aloud whether humanity will ever receive the message. "The "pandemic is a portal," says Arundhati Roy. It is the most oft-cited high-theoretical phrase circulating amongst the professional-class mainstream, but we seem to be at a loss when it comes to understanding what it would actually take to walk through. The new bourgeoise know about obligatory nods—land acknowledgements, check-in questions about how the pandemic has "changed" you, and solidarity statements with Black Lives Matter. We seem to have missed the message that our entire way of life must be surrendered to answer the question the pandemic is asking.

SKiNFoLK is the one road to such a surrender—surrendering to a world that does not so deeply rely on anti-Black violence to keep spinning. Where, in the cutting words of the piece, "the African American experience is [being a thread] that holds everything in place." Walker takes us through the necessary unraveling of her line of this infinitely long thread inside the African American experience. If we travel long enough, or even if we travel well, we have the chance to unravel our own in the process. We must remember, no matter how uncomfortable it gets, that this is a necessary displacement (a Black map is, after all, a map of undoing). This quality of multi-vocality—the I, the you, the we, the us, the they, the them, all being wrapped up together in this spirit working—translates into the plethora of ways the work can also shapeshift in form.

There are infinite possibilities to receive SKiNFoLK—in text, in performance, in song, in concert, in album. There are possibilities on possibility. No matter which form you encounter, Walker, who reminisces on her own last name and her line's attendant gift of "taking the next step forward," takes you, (for you are thought of, written into this work) on a journey with a "bad band" and her sister/kin into a time-space continuum where quantum physics and Afro-Indigenous knowledge meet:

the jook joint   under the roots   middle passage ocean   braiding shop   concert

In this world, HERE is inevitably multiple, and Walker, in alignment with other Black artists of our time, re-imagines these portals for Black embodied knowledge as "theatre," with the same, high stakes of the Greek "seeing place." It is HERE, in this multiplied, palimpsest of a place, that the lineages of Blackness in the United States can be observed with sharpness, humor, grief, play, and hard truth.

Walker is a deeply capable guide. She and her sistren tell you everything you need to know, when you need to know it. They'll keep orienting you. It's an act of care, and an act of wisdom—this moving, embodied navigation that places you multiply, where the you is multiple, the where is multiple, and so is the when. One can never be too certain about these things, as the Middle Passage churns in our next moments as well as the ones that have passed. It churns everytime a Black person is shot inside an extra-judicial moment of quelling a God particle as it manifests in a Black body, and Kanyé's and De'Anna's God-dreams turn to American nightmares while we still learn our lessons, so many of them on the backs of God's body. "We go down," in that way too. But we also Get Down, like James Brown and the infamous break that birthed break-dance and its trifecta counter-parts, hip-hop and graffiti—art, joy, possibility spilling out all over the world. We still get down twerking and line-dancing it out at block parties, family reunions, jazz clubs, and intimate dinners, cuz we fancy too. Black embodiment is the saving grace, always. And Black spirit is eternal. It's all here. Churning in these pages and movements.

o

Miss Walker's gonna tell you some things. And if I were you, I would listen. Ear to the ground, heart drumming into the below. If you do, I can't promise you what kind of remembering you'll find, only that you gon' learn today. Something about you, something about her, something about us, us skinfolk, which is another way of saying the force that animates life on this planet, which is another way of saying you'll learn something about the place you call home. Maybe to see it different, hear it different, smell it different, know it different. This is not a work for running away. It's a work for going down down down together. Your fear will not serve you here, but don't worry. Going down feels so good.

And when it doesn't, you'll learn something about the part of you that roars in the night. Ready to face any and all things that would come between you and your destiny. This is history, herstory, theirstory, ourstory woven through with the plight of Black women—cafe con leche to dark chocolate. Our bloodlines, our wonderings and wanderings, the ways we feel prison and the ways we feel free. In our bodies, on our bodies, all up on our bodies.

This is a mapping. If you want a key, read carefully. I mean read with your bones. I mean, if you can help it, don't read at all. Just let your eyes arrive. It's not a doing, it's a stepping in. Take breaks. Drink water. Dance. Read it to a lover. Read it to a grandmother. Read it to a child. Read it to a class. Be together with it and in it. Or just listen to the sounds. Listen to the waves. Let them wash you. Call you. Free you. Remember you.

It feels important to say that this work oozes jazz. Oozes swing. Oozes classic R&B. All that to say, as you read it, do not doubt for one second that it too is reading you. Walker beckons you to sit beside her at the mirror. And the mirror goes both ways.

– Nia O. Witherspoon

SHOW NOTES

There are various American traditions that intersect and weave into and out of many, many other traditions. This show is focused on accessing the power and magic of Black Southern and Great Migration traditions in the United States. These places include, but are not limited to: Lowcountry, the Delta, Gullah Geechee, and the Chesapeake with significant migrations northward to Detroit, Chicago, Cleveland, St. Louis, Philadelphia, and New York, to name a few. Black women who have experience(s) inside of these traditions and kin in these traditions can access these characters through the portal of ancestry and legacy. There is nothing to put on in this performance (unless you want to). Find it inside. Use it. You already wear your own skin.

It follows, then, that stage directions containing ritual are suggestions—guidelines, of sorts. This work is designed to leave space for the bodies that inhabit it and the team that surrounds it, meaning that the ritual will be different depending on who's inside of it, meaning:

Be with each;

Find the synergy that is unique to the performers, only found by those performers. Use gesture and movement. Ad lib and weave a tapestry of COLLECTIVE MEANING-MAKING. If that ain't America, I'm not sure where we are.

LANGUAGE NOTES

[Brackets indicate text that is organically shared between ME, AVERY, and SMILING TUXEDOED MAN, not necessarily in unison, but in a rapid echo style. Think jazz. Or the praise and worship team at Church.]

Scattered words
        also read like jazz.

{Braced words and lines throughout can be loosely shared by the performers in terms of rhythm. **Bolded words** should be shared in unison. Braces also have a different emotional meaning and visual impact than brackets.}

| Words in columns are spoken simultaneously. | Words in columns are spoken simultaneously. |

Stage directions that feel right to the performers can be read aloud because this is, among other things, a play about performance.

.   A moment to build, establish, or feel for TRUST.

:   A longer moment, a breath, a shift moving us forward in trust.

Capitalization is sometimes used for emphasis, or to decolonize a thought, a phrase, to provide a physical and psychic disruption, or to introduce sacred items or elements (the Sun, the Water, Jerricans, etc.). All of these are invitations for consideration in performance, design, and direction.

Punctuation is used as part of the felt-sense reality of identity. YOU v you, Black v black. Sometimes these are emphasized and sometimes deemphasized and that's on purpose.

CHARACTERS

YOU—Yes, you. Whoever and however you are.

ME—Yeah. Me. Black, female–plus…♭

A ♭AD ♭AND—A Bad. Ass. Band. (preferably *full* keys, drums, bass, and guitar. Even better with a couple of strings and a horn or two). The Band has names:

    Francis—Keys
    Pipsy—Drums
    Rollo—Bass
    Jovetta—Guitar

And a couple of ancestors:

AVERY NOLASTNAME—A mythical "light-skinned" starlet. Think Dorothy D., Lena, a bit of Janet, and some Yonce all on his mouth like…She's a glamorous, glamorous drunk—like Billie!—with a killer voice that she actually uses to try to kill members of her global audiences, though it has yet to work. Must have strong musicality, and always an heir/air of unpredictability. Possibly the God Particle. Very strong singer. Good with harmonies. Black. Woman.

SMILING TUXEDOED MAN / NIXON—Another part of the God Particle. A woman with tremendous gravitas. Mystery. A charismatic navigator, host, and bringer of information who transforms into Richard Nixon when SHe feels like it. Why? Who knows?—SHe does. A player playing with YOUr expectations perhaps a bit darkly, dubiously, but ultimately for YOUr own good. Also must be a strong singer. Good with harmonies. Black, femme-of-center/tearing "the center" toward femme.

MOVEMENTS

Prelude: The Incantation of the Joint

Movement 1: The Descent

Movement 2: Unpacking Blackness

Movement 3: Meet the SKiNFoLK

Movement 4: Unbelonging

Movement 5: Fall Apart

Movement 6: Reclamation

SONGS

We Go Down ALL // What Does My Blackness Have to do With You ALL // I Can't Do it Anymore AVERY // African American ME // Black is the Color of Everything Combined ALL // Call to My Next of Kin ME // Portal to the Roots ME // Some of You Are Drunk ALL // The Ruler of All Things Real ME // Kerosene ALL // Jerrican ALL // While the Sun Waits ALL

TIME

Is.

PLACE

A jOok joint, with YOU. The roots and under the roots of a tree. The middle passage. The ocean. A braiding shop. A concert.

SOUND

Envelops and immerses us on the ground.

The Incantation of the Joint

A SMILING TUXEDOED MAN *enters with a*
silver tray of neon sippies. Smiles.

ME
Follow me
YOU follow me through low-hanging roots. And—
Hands open some vines to clear your path
Hands hands more hands
And
YOU are in an arched hallway—limestone. Whitewashed. Clean lines. YOU
walk and walk forward.
YOU hear
Nothing.
Nothing.

Water surrounds your ankles.

BAD BAND *plays like water*
waater

YOU keep walking down the hallway.

.

.

.

Setting:

ME
A hole? A cave? A portal. A *portal* underneath the roots of a tree. Mahogany,
cinnamon, cacao dirt surrounds YOU. Roots weave in and around YOU—
some the shade of ginger, some darker like—clove. All warm, enveloping.
YOU feel safe. Protected. Able, perhaps, to go to sleep in a nearby tangle,
though YOU will not because YOU are excited to be in this place.

{ALL}
To see.

AVERY

It all looks delicious. Even the Earthworms undulating in the cayenne-caked walls are sexy. Are YOU attracted to Earthworms?—And rollie pollies: here, they relax, stretching out each plate. No need to keep themselves tied up tight like they must above the surface. No, here, it is all well and good to be shell-less and out of control of their segmented parts.

SMILING TUXEDOED MAN

There are tables and tablecloths—white. Small, round tables that make room for dates, new and old, and all kinds of romances: with touch, smell, with light and sound. With whomever YOU may meet tonight.

ME

YOU are in a jook joint. A classy jooky joint.

.

.

.

.

Glass mason jars sit at every table, glowing a soft light. YOU may think the light is giggling it's so bubbly about somehow getting air underground, in this dirt, in this portal. It's so happy. Elegant Jerricans lantern the space. Inside some of these containers YOU see fireflies. Fireflies? Yes, fireflies. The American Southern kind. Or the Midwest ones. For sure, a part of the country forgotten by most streetlamps and reflective traffic drums. Pre-filament fireflies. Other jerricans around YOU contain magic light that look like laughing candles, but they aren't. They're someone's country kitchen secret. Burnin pig fat? But there's no smell, just a soft yellow glow.

SMILING TUXEDOED MAN
YOU *taste*
YOU taste…!

{ALL}
Movement one: the Descent.

MOVEMENT 1:

The
Descent

> BAD BAND *starts groovin on "We Go Down."*
>
> Before too long a stage appears. A stage.
> A
> *Stage.*

SMILING TUXEDOED MAN
The BAND, the BAND!!! A BAD BAND appears.
The BADDEST BAND–*ass* BAD, the-good-kind-of-bad. Tina-Turner-Rosetta-Tharpe-bad. Anita-Baker-bad. Aretha-Franklin-Nina-Simone-bad-Odetta-bad-witchy-Badu-bad. Sade BAD. Yes, that BAD. Francis! Pipsy! *Rollo*!

> *We go down*
> *We go down*
> *We go down together*
>
> *We go down*
> *We go down*
> *We go down together*
>
> *Hey hey together*
> *Together we go down*
> *Dontcha know*
>
> *Hey hey together*
> *Together we go down*

SMILING TUXEDOED MAN
More setting:

BAD BAND is crucial to everything. The magic of the whole night. Where they came from, how they got here, who knows. Another portal? Other-worldly sound suggests, but no one can be sure. No matter what or who may get confused tonight, BAD BAND plays on.

We go round
We go round
We go round together

We go round
We go round
We go round together

Hey hey together
Together we go round
Dontcha know

Hey hey together
Together we go round

We go down
We go down
We go down together

We go down
We go down
We go down together

Hey hey together
Together we go down
Hey hey together
Together we go down

SMILING TUXEDOED MAN
Pass down the middle
Pass down the middle, please
Won't you pass down the middle?

Middle pass Middle
Pass middle
Pass
Pass
Passing?
P
Pass

Middle pass
Puh.
middle—

YOU pass down the middle.

YOU pass and YOU pass
and
YOU see a sign that reads *"Please hand her a bobby pin at your leisure."*

ME
YOU feel anxious

AVERY
YOU wonder if you remember what a bobby pin is.
:
A bobby pin?

SMILING TUXEDOED MAN
You don't wanna be wrong.

ME
Bobby pin, safety
Bobby pin, safety
Which one is the right one in your mind?

SMILING TUXEDOED MAN
YOU walk further in.

        AVERY
        YOU see a table filled with tools and hair devices:

SMILING TUXEDOED MAN
YOU see a hot comb on a burned white towel

        AVERY
        YOU see snapping barrettes of

                ME
                multiple colors, rainbows, myth-
                ical creatures

SMILING TUXEDOED MAN
{you see}

        AVERY
        YOU see two balled barrettes of gold and of silver

                SMILING TUXEDOED MAN
                {you see}

AVERY
And zoo animals.

        ME
        YOU see silver metal industrial duck mouth hair
        clips

      SMILING TUXEDOED MAN
      YOU see blow drier parts—tubes, cords.

           AVERY
           {you see}

SMILING TUXEDOED MAN
YOU see tiny black rubber bands

        ME
        YOU see tiny transparent rubber bands

   AVERY
   YOU see big bobby pins

        SMILING TUXEDOED MAN
        YOU see small bobby pins

        ME
        ǝɯ ǝǝs UOY

       ɹoɹɹᴉɯ ɐ ʇɐ

ME
I come toward YOU
Walking through water, too
I say:
I'm not supposed to talk about this
Until my grandmother is dead
She's not dead
She's very much in Michigan
Attending Kiwanis meetings
And sorority boules

But since I hope she lives long enough to meet my children
     (And that maybe won't be for a while, maybe)
And since I came into some good good genes

With great-grandmothers who knitted me quilts and told me stories and
looked at me with wonder-rimmed eyes
Dresses passed down
Smiles
And particular pronunciations of words
Because I am ME
And you are YOU
And we are US.
I'm gonna talk about it now
I'm gonna tell it now
Because my skinfolk gave me this story
And hopefully my grandmother won't be mad
And the skinfolk who've been silent
While the other ones yell over each other inside me
Won't be too mad

.

.

.

The greatest war a granddaughter can wage
Is the one where she tries to make everybody happy
And buries all her own whispers
in the folds of her tongue

I roar mine through the lining of my throat
And hope for the best outcome
For yes it remains that
my greatest fear is being a bad granddaughter,
Yes.

I look at YOU
YOU look

> SMILING TUXEDOED MAN *collects bobby
> pins from* YOU, *like Sunday Offering.
> Meanwhile,* BAD BAND *plays a New Orle-
> ans funeral march version of "Blackness."*
> ME *puts them in her hair, pinning it up
> in an elaborate-looking updo. Then—*
>
> *Beat.*
>
> *Beat.*

ME
YOU like?

> *I am the greatest myth*
> *That ever lived*
> *Ever lived*
> *Ever lived*
>
> *And you*
> *When you speak my name*
> *I watch your lips*
> *Watch your lips*
> *Watch your lips*
>
> *I was around before Plato*
> *I was alive before time*
> *I was defined before nothing*
> *So you can't recall me in your mind*
> *All the attempts to contain me*
> *Don't make it none but too far*
> *No matter how far the light stretches*
> *Forever I'll be right nearby*
>
> *What does my blackness have to do with you*
> *Boo boo*
> *Boo*
> *Boo boo boo*
> *Boo boo*
> *Boo boo*
>
> *What does my blackness have to do with you*
> *Boo boo*
> *Boo*
> *Boo boo boo*
> *Boo boo*
>
> *Hey*
> *Hey hey hey*
> *Hey hey hey*
> *Hey hey hey*
> *Hey hey hey*
> *Hey hey hey*

Hey hey hey
Hey hey hey

SMILING TUXEDOED MAN
The hallway, the *hallway*,
YOU hear voices now.

{ALL}
curves

AVERY
YOU see figures of women

{ALL}
curves

SMILING TUXEDOED MAN
YOU hear the figures talking
YOU hear

ME
A List of Weapons:

SMILING TUXEDOED MAN
A mouse trap,
tiny nunchucks,
land mines,
AK47,
ICBMs: intercontinental ballistic missiles.

Beat.

Lipstick.
Stilettos—both on and off the feet.
A baby stroller. A mother pushing a baby stroller.
Mimosas, sassy, nappy, snappy, feminist.
　　"Bless your heart"
　　"Bless your heart"
　　"Bless your heart."
You hear songs about hoes, you hear songs about niggers. You hear songs about niggers fucking hoes. You hear the word fuck. You feel shrapnel, bullets, NYPD officers, Ferguson officers, LAPD officers, any officers who are afraid of black people which is pretty much all of them. Even the black officers.

{ALL}
You think about over-simplification. You think about over-sophistication: high-saddity surviving. You see the Atom-bomb over Hiroshima and Nagasaki—how that doesn't come up more baffles you. How short our memories are astounds you. This happened, that happened in real life to real people. We vow never to forget 9/11 and maybe we shouldn't, but it seems unfair to you that we've forgotten Hiroshima and Nagasaki: Hands. You feel hands. Eyes. You feel cut. You feel broken a million times. You smell chemicals, medicines, anthrax–space junk. You feel leather whips... hot oil, skillet heat, a barbecue skewer. You see a candlestick in the library, a wrench in the parlor, "if it don't fit, you must a–", you hear a set of keys. You hear your mother. You feel a bath that's too hot. You see your own mind. Filtering itself, over and over.

> BAD BAND *begins a reprise of "Blackness"*
> *in the background.*

ME
You feel really cold water, you jump.

SMILING TUXEDOED MAN
You hear a pair of dangly earrings,

> ME
> a fallen tree, a burning fire, a willow branch.

> AVERY
> You taste a piece of coral dried out in the sun, you
> lick a swing-set, a bucket of sand.

> ME
> You feel patent leather shoes that are too tight. Scissors.

> AVERY
> You see scissors you used to keep under your pillow to
> cut the tape and suck your thumb.

> ME
> You hear people laughing. Laughter. You think about prisons.

> BAND *break.*

SMILING TUXEDOED MAN
YOU see the end of the hallway
YOU fixate on that end. Is it time for a sippie-sippie?

*BAD BAND plays the full reprise of "Black-
ness." ALL sing in a round with hotcombs
for mics:*

What does my AFRO *have to do with you*

What does my WORMHOLE *have to do with you*

What does my MAGIC *have to do with you*

What does my LACEFRONT *have to do with you*

What does my HAIRGEL *have to do with you*

What does my ACCENT *have to do with you*

What does my SUBURB *have to do with you*

{ALL}
What does my PROJECT *have to do with you*
Boo boo boo
Boo boo boo boo boo boo boo, etc.

BAD BAND outro while ...

*ME pulls out a mason jar, glowing with
light. ME toasts YOU and drinks the light.*

MOVEMENT 2:

Unpacking
Blackness

SMILING TUXEDOED MAN
In their competition for sunlight, trees evolved a way to defy gravity. Before trees, the highest vegetation was only about waist-high and then something wonderful happened
:

A plant molecule evolved that was both strong, and flexible; a material that could support a lot of weight, yet bend in the wind without breaking.

Beat.

ME
I am one-hundred percent African-American.
Which means
Which means what?

When you're "African" and "American"
people usually want to know what you're mixed with
especially if you look like me
A billowy high yellowy carmely sect of skinburnt sun
Dripped over lean bones
And people usually want to know what you're mixed with
so that that can become the topic of discussion
so that you can talk about the Indian part
or the Bajan part
or the German part
you become more interesting, ya see
because everyone already thinks they know
everyone thinks they know your story
when you're african american
unless you're Creole or
one of your parents is from Jamaica
It is then they may lean in,
They may tip their chin
They may hmmm, interesting–cock

Something to exotify the black looking back at them

Otherwise it's:
"my great great great grandaddies were slaves
and then they were practically slaves
and then they were mud-poor
and then they were a little, little less than mud-poor
and then they were dust poor
and then there was the projects
and then there was the suburbs
And den dey wasuh slaves to da capitalism
slaves to da capitalism
slaves to da capitalism
Lism lism lism lism…"

Nobody's leaning in for that.

> BAD BAND *plays a creepy, jazzy version of "Hail to the Chief." Someone is out of key?*

> SMILING TUXEDOED MAN *transforms into a black woman's version of* RICHARD NIXON, *shaking hands as she goes:*

SMILING TUXEDOED MAN / NIXON
(Like the movie trailer guy) In a world …where blackness is everything—and *nothing*.

> *Beat.*

Naaaaaawwwww! Ladies, Gentleman, Those of All Genders and Semi-genders, welcome to the party! Tonight, we have a special guest—rare, like actual grassfedmeatcan'tbebeatwhatatreat. We're not gonna eat her raw, though. No, no. Tonight. Tonight we will Cook her, slowly under these lights til she's brown and tender. *Browner.*

> *He snaps his fingers. No lights come on. Tries again. No. Recovers:*

Tonight we will eat her in parts—delicious parts: devouring Legs, Eyes, her Wings—*If* we can get to their meat. *I am your host, Richard Nixon, your guide, your trusted ally. Please put your hands together for your well of entertainment, your favorite piece of joy: Averyyyyyy Nolastnaaaaame!*

AVERY

So lovely, so lovely *so* lovely to be here tonight.

Smiley beat.

You know, I was born in Natchez, Mississippi. Right near the river. I came from the river, actually, just emerged. Me and the Mississippi the same color.

AVERY *drinks!*

AVERY *pins up her hair.*

I was—Am? Was-Am! Was named after my great-grandfather: Avery Clifford Beauxregard. A fighter in the confederate army and upholder of the peculiar institution. "How peculiar!" you might think, considering—she runs her hands along her body—hahahahaha! Well, nevertheless he fell in love and promptly broom-jumped with a freewoman named Sadie and that made my grandmomma who then made my mother and uncles and thangs that then made me. And here, here I am! On this stage and ACB (that's what I call 'im: A-C-B) would think, I think he would think, he has never seen such a glorious thing before in his life. Me! On this stage. For all of—with all of YOU. My true joy in life is performing for YOU.

BAD BAND *begins the neo-souly mid-tempo romp, "I Can't Do It Anymore."*

This is one I wrote for my ex-husband, Claude. He was 30% Swiss.

> *I wish I could go*
> *Where I wanna go*
> *Do what I would do*
> *Still stay true to you*
> *But*
> *I can't do it anymore*
>
> *I don't wanna know*
> *Where you wanna go*
> *I just want you*
> *To show up and be true*
> *Oh*
> *I can't do it anymore*
>
> *I'm tired of lies*
> *On your side and mine*

I just know
That I don't wanna do it anymore

I'm tired of trying halfway
And getting far enough to know
That you and I have gotta make a change

(Gotta make a change)

I just wanna know
Where I gotta go
Still I want you
To show up and be true
Oh
But I can't do it anymore

I just wanna fly
High up in the sky
Still I want you
To show up and be true
Oh
I can't do it anymore

I can't do it anymore
I can't do it anymore
I can't do it anymore
I can't do it anymore

AVERY
As Zora Neale Hurston wrote:
"I feel most colored when I am thrown against a stark white background."
Stark?

ME
Sharp.
Sharp white background.

ME + AVERY
Ya see, ya see, ya see. People don't understand. The difficulty. Because everything's sposed to be equal now you see. And I'm pretty! Which is sposed to cancel out everything. But it don't—*doesn't* it does not cancel out everything. *Anything.* I was blacklisted—

AVERY *bows. She's a little drunk so it's an event.*

AVERY
you see. For—the list is all black. The blacklist is black. It has something to do with me being from Mississippi and I have—had—*have* the wrong kind of accent, I think.

SMILING TUXEDOED MAN
Is she a hostage? YOU feel uncomfortable. YOU want to help her. Or, YOU are already consuming her, just like everyone else, YOU can't see her.

SMILING TUXEDOED MAN / NIXON
One more time for Avery! She'll be back in all her deliciousity after a short scotch break.

ME
...and there might be, yes there might be some Native American in my family the favorite myth of 88.8% African-American families
all claiming one shared Cherokee ancestor we keep a picture of on our eldest family member's mantle
Cherokee being the only tribe black people remember
((The nation))
22% of the time
It's the Navajo
rare:
Ojibway
Choctaw
Lakota

Who are still here
All Very much still here

But, the Cherokee—
To those sisters and brothers we cling
Our one hope out of blackity blackness
Anything to get away from black
Away from that color
That oil
That leaks onto
Clear pristine waters
Sits and sinks its shameful shade
Onto everything
We sit
Away from shame

We try.

I gave em what
They asked me for
They want my name
I tell em so:

"It's not enough
To keep afloat
You'll drown in anonymity
You'll never quite fly
What do you mean
You're just a Brown?
A Thompson or a Jenkins
Or a Davis or a Jones?
A Jones a Jones a Jones

Feel sorry for your history
But I don't wanna hear about your misery
And I don't wanna hear about it cause it's all your fault"

Don't know what to do
I gave them what they asked me for
So it's time to leave respectable outside the door
And I do my best I'm askin you
Why can't this life just be real easy?

I'm so sick and tired of doing other people's work
But my freedom makes me lean into the deepest lurch
And I'm askin you
To join me
But why seems like
You don't wanna hear me

Seems like you don't wanna hear me?

You want my hair
You want my vibe
Then turn around and call me ugly to the side

The kinda stuff
We dealin wit

It makes me wanna fall down but instead I lift
I lift myself high
I lift myself real high
I reach for the light
Reaching for the light

Don't know what to do
I gave them what they ask me for
So it's time to leave respectable outside the door
And I do my best I'm tellin you
Why can't this life just be real easy?

I'm so sick and tired of doing other people's work
But my freedom makes me lean into the deepest lurch
And I'm askin you
To join me
But why seems like
You don't wanna hear me

Seems like you don't wanna hear me?

When the sun sets overhead
Keep in mind til morningtime
I'm blendin in
I'm blendin in
And that's cuz I'm an African-American

When the sun sets overhead
Keep in mind til morningtime
I'm blendin in
I'm blendin in
And that's cuz I'm an African-American

Jazz swing breakdown.

ME
There are parts of skinfolk
planning to come back for other parts
when the smoke settles
when the shame dissipates
but it never does
and so we never come back
we don't

shame is black smoke
And sprayed soot
That grows over so thick
hardens and refuses to budge
and all I can do to keep breathin
is push
push on
push away
work
work on
work toward
play
play on
don't stop
keep on movin
don't stop no
don't look back

> *Black is the color of everything combined*
> *Black is the color of everything combined*
>
> *Live in the darkness and be all right*
> *Black is the color of everything combined*
>
> *Black is the color of everything combined*
> *Black is the color of everything combined*
>
> *The blacker the berry, the sweeter the vine*
> *Black is the color of everything combined*
>
> *Black is the color of everything combined*
> *Black is the color of everything combined*
>
> *We make you look for our magic inside*
> *Black is the color of everything combined*

ME
YOU and ME have a disco party. YOU drink, YOU laugh.

YOU forget things.

> *What sits on top of the dash*
> *(top-of-the-dash)*
> *(top-of-the-dash)*

Maybe nothing maybe all
maybe nothin maybe
Top-of-the-dash
(top-of-the-dash)
(top-of-the-dash)

Maybe nothing

What sits on top of the dash
(top-of-the-dash)
(top-of-the-dash)
Maybe nothing maybe all
Maybe nothing maybe
(top-of-the-dash)
(top-of-the-dash)
(top-of-the-dash))

Maybe all

ME

But light-skinned girls don't feel no pain

{ALL}

But light-skinned girls don't feel no pain
We shine like the sun
And fend off the rain

Light-skinned girls don't feel no pain
Hey hey hey
Look at me
Hey hey hey
Isn't she
Isn't she

So—!!!!!

Black is the color of everything combined
Black is the color of everything combined

The blacker the berry, the sweeter the vine
Black is the color of everything combined

SMILING TUXEDOED MAN
Enjoy more food and drink.

SMILING TUXEDOED MAN *is a great host.*
The best.

{ALL}

.

.

ME
My black friends too quick to point out where they
        Ain't black
Because their great grandmother wore her good hair in pigtails

                    SMILING TUXEDOED MAN
                    So she was definitely Indian
AVERY
Or their Grandaddies' People from Baton Rouge and the last name Creole

ME
Last Name
                    SMILING TUXEDOED MAN
                    Last Name

AVERY
Name

                                        ME
                                        Last name

SMILING TUXEDOED MAN
Not black not black nooo, not black

            AVERY
            Not-a-black-name
                            (Microbreath)

ME
Or the slave that was freed
that willingly married the white man and lived
happily cabinned after
These folks too quick to point it out

.

.

AVERY
I'm not not black I'm from the islands, BUT—

SMILING TUXEDOED MAN
I'm not black I'm

AVERY
My grandfather was

ME
My people

SMILING TUXEDOED MAN
We have

AVERY
I'm Puerto Rican

ME
We traced our line to

AVERY
We not black

SMILING TUXEDOED MAN
No I'm not black
:
:

{ALL}
I'm

SMILING TUXEDOED MAN
I'm

ME
I'm a moor

SMILING TUXEDOED MAN
I'm

AVERY
I'm post-racial

SMILING TUXEDOED MAN
I'm new

ME
I'm a human

AVERY
I'm Red Pill, Blue Pill.

ME
I'm

AVERY
I'm staying right here in the Matrix

SMILING TUXEDOED MAN
I'm not into that
You go alone

ME
Come back to the mirror with me
Link your onyx arm
Around mine and stand
Next to me

:

Please.

> *This is a call to my next of kin*
> *This is a call to my next of kin*
> *Do you know whose skin you live in?*
> *Do you know whose skin you live in?*
> *In in in in in*
> *In in in in in?*

Meet *the* SKiNFoLK

ME
This is my great-grandmother.

ME
This is my great-grandmother.

SMILING TUXEDOED MAN
What to do with all those dead trees.
It took the fungi and bacteria
Millions of years to evolve the biochemical means
To consume them
Meanwhile
The trees just kept springing up
Falling
Dying over
And getting buried by the mud that built up over eons.
.

Eventually
There were hundreds of billions of trees
Entombed in the Earth
Buried forests
All over the earth.

ME *(blues)*
>*Once*
>*When I was little*
>*I spent the night at my grandmother's house*
>*The sun shined in through her chantilly curtains*
>*The next morning*
>*It was hot*
>
>*I woke up*
>*And stepped my foot right out of the bed*
>*And onto a blade of glass*
>*That's what this feels like*

{ALL}
>*To see the Sun!*

ME
To see the sun
And think it's gonna be a gloryfull day
And before there can be a next thought
There's a shard of glass

{ALL}
Embedded
In the bottom of your foot

SMILING TUXEDOED MAN
Dripping communion blood onto the matching red carpet

AVERY
You're frozen
So

ME
You haven't thought it's *not* gonna be a good day
You haven't had the chance to think

AVERY
Or forget the sun

ME
But you're bleeding and that's taking up your time now.

ME
This is my great-great grandfather.

June 22, 1947
Left to Right: Rev. H. F. Donnelly, John Hinson, R. A. Jackson, Jim Jackson, Elmer McAleer,
(partly hidden), Rev. Posey, Charlie Hinson, Archie Jackson and Josh Jackson

ME
And this is my great-great grandfather.

My Loving Father
W M Wood

ME

Go in the portal to the roots
Let em breathe with ya
Go in the portal to the roots
Make em bleed with ya
Go in the portal to the roots
Let em be with ya
Go in the portal to the roots
Let em breathe with ya
I look at YOU
YOU *look*
I look at YOU
You look

I look at YOU
YOU *look*
YOU *look*

SMILING TUXEDOED MAN
When plants die they decay and this reverses the transaction. Their organic matter combines with oxygen and decomposes, putting carbon dioxide back into the air. This balances the books for the chemistry of earth's atmosphere. But if the trees are buried before they can decay, two things happen: they take the carbon and stored solar energy with them and leave the oxygen behind to build up in the atmosphere.

ME
A few years back, my parents took one of those
DNA tests
African ancestry thingies
a valiant effort to recover rituals
Long-lost on the Atlantic bottom

There's some Igbo (in my family)
and some Irish roots much to my father's horror
Since the Irish are white—now.

We can't find the results
Those things were not locked up in the safe
where we keep our American passports
They probably got thrown away
Or my father burned them.

It'd be nice to have some numbers
math
grounds things in the world
this material statistical space
We're all obsessed with creating
where we freely start conversations with: "I'm fifty percent Thai, thirty
percent Hungarian and twenty percent bored with you."
I rely on
the less statistical—
No percentages—
less real, I guess
the ephemeral
the abstract
the might have been
could have been
likely was.

I do have one number:
I am 85% stored with grief.
Which is hard to justify.

.

.

.

We had a three-car garage.

ME
John. And Anner.
JohnanAnner. Walker.
Willie Maude Smart.
Louise (Lucy) Woods
Archie "Pa" Jackson.
WM Woods.

AVERY *on a talk show with* RICHARD
NIXON. *She's dressed in a '70s disco
jumpsuit. She and* NIXON *use hot combs
as microphones and a hot comb stove as
a microphone stand.*

The whole cast makes the laughtrack.

AVERY

(Laughing maniacally) Well, Dick, I was born in Lebanon during a very sexy persecution. Hahahahaha! My halfJewishhalfIrish part South Indian mother whisked us off to Bangladesh while my father stayed behind in Java to take care of his mother who is part Balinese and part Swedish. My father? My father is 15% Lithuanian 10% Croatian and 35% western Himalayan. Oh, and he's 23% emotionally available.

> *Audience laughter and applause. Cast laughs and applauds.*

I'm brown because when we came to the United States I tripped over the tip of Manhattan and my body hit the liberty bell and my bruise never quite healed. It's sexy to be from somewhere, iddn't it? Isn't tit, haha! I mean.

> *She laughs slowly at first. She laughs and laughs. Harder. Harder. She laughs.* AVERY *scans* YOU, *looking out at* YOU. *She says to* YOU:

Where are you from darling?
City or country?

> *She waits.*

Mmmmmmm.
But where are you *from?*

Your people, they're from ...?

> *She waits.*

How lovely.

And where are you from
In your Bones.
You're from _____
Don't think.
Sit.
Listen. In your bones.
You're from _____.

Now,
I'm gonna borrow from church for a minute

> BAD BAND *plays a baptist fellowship song.*

ME, NIXON, *and* BAD BAND *fellowship
with folks in the joint. Praise and praise!
The place fills with—connection. With
harmony.*

Though Lord forgive me
I haven't been to church since it was excusable to wear lace
Round the top of my socks
Ahahahahahahahahahaha! She takes a drink.
Now, turn to your neighbor now
Turn to your neighbor
And tell them where you are from.
Now, shake hands.

YOU *do.*

Now, how was that?
Fun?
Terrifying?
Something else?
Well, have a drink to celebrate!

ME
We have a Praise Break. A calling in. A—is this a summoning? We dance.
We praise. We dance until we're not sure whether we are alive or dead.
Whether this is real. Is this theater? Are we performing? What is "perfor-
mance" to us? What is worship?

Suddenly, a Gregorian chant:

{ALL}
    Some of you are drunk and you think you hear angels
    Some of you are drunk and you think you hear angels
    Some of you are drunk and you think you hear angels

    Can you hear angels?
    Think you hear angels
    Can you hear angels?
    Think you hear angels

    Can you hear angels?
    Think you hear angels

MOVEMENT 4:

Unbelonging

I've been to the ocean many times
The Atlantic Ocean
Maine
(skip the vineyard)
(skip the outer banks)
Virginia Beach
Hilton Head
(skip gullah)
Florida

Never much paid attention to what I was rubbin against
Or what was rubbin gainst me
Never much paid much attention.

When I was twelve
I was stung by a jellyfish—
A regular one.
Just spawning season.
I didn't know then,
Things needed to come close to shore to mate
to be with one another
Huggin on the shore
In their way.

I just played and played
Squealin and squallin around in the waves
And I got stung.
I thought
Somethin had ripped through my flesh
Coral,
Or—

But it was just barbs of poison
that in the end
didn't do too much.

It hurt
for a moment
And once I got a hold of what was happening—
in my mind I mean,
I saw that they had been there
Everywhere
Jellyfish all over the beach
the whole time
They had told me they were there
plumply huggin and blubber just blurting through the sand.

I just didn't see them until
I had been effected
Until I had been hurt
I just didn't see them until
It mattered.
They're not my favorite animal:
I like the sabertooth tiger!
But I respect all creatures of the sea
And we still don't know all
the things that's in there.

ME
Family trees look neat
Knotted in the right places

{ALL}
But this is how they feel

SMILING TUXEDOED MAN + {ALL}
The process of how a tree takes water is thus

> *Looks it up in a dusty book that falls
> from the roof of the joint:*

{Water} mostly enters a {tree} through the roots by osmosis and any dissolved
mineral nutrients will travel with it upward through the inner bark's xylem
(using capillary action) and into the leaves. These travelling nutrients then
feed the {tree} through the process of leaf photosynthesis.

These travelling nutrients then feed the {tree} through the process of leaf photosynthesis.

Photosynthesis *(a photo album falls)* is the process by which plants, *(looking it up)* some bacteria, and some protestants, oops! *PRO-TI-STANS* use the energy from sunlight to produce sugar, which cellular respiration converts into ATP, the "fuel" used by all living things.

    {ALL}
    We breathe.

SMILING TUXEDOED MAN
Protistans
Protistans *(laughs)*

> SMILING TUXEDOED MAN *takes a tiny book from a mason jar.*

Related: *Protists.* Protists are the members of an informal grouping of diverse eukaryotic organisms that are not animals, plants or fungi. They do not form a natural group, or clade, but are often grouped together for convenience, like algae or invertebrates.

ME
We wonder:
Do Protists *protest?*
Do they protest
their grouping of convenience—
like the algae?

The Kongo
who didn't know the Serer
Before they were joined in a bed of
Algae
Algae
Atlantic Algae
Too tired, proud, or manacled to work for strangers
To labor on strangers
With strangers
For strangers
deciding to rest in the Algae
Algae
that does not form a natural group, or clade,
but is often grouped together for convenience

Like
the Protists
and
Invertebrates.

Trees
look
very neat.
With their regal rings
and their ranging wrangling that gives us just the right kind of shade
But they have dying branches
and they have sugar addictions just like us—
to get to fan out in the sun
And be themselves.

AVERY
Write this down: "The African-American experience is:
{Being a **thread**}
that holds
Everything
In place.
{Being the **sound**}
that draws
itself out
Across The World
{**An answer**}
An experience
that
no one has asked
The right questions for.

ME
I walk
With my head turned slightly up and to the left.
Because I'm usually afraid someone
is going to tell me I don't belong there
There
There
Even when I have a key

Making eye contact
I hold my breath
Still

I feel the sound coming in
That says I am in the wrong place

I hold my chin a little higher
And I smirk.

I walk around with a backpack of water
I barely drink
But it's there in case
There's no There
there
Or I get stuck underground
On the train
Trying to get "home."

.
.
.

Black feels compressed to me—
Like Shale.
Whatever that mother tongue was—
The bottom layer.

> *Even* YOU *feel lost to me sometimes. Even*
> *you.*
>
> RICHARD NIXON *spins his chair around,*
> ME *sits.* AVERY *mimes braiding:*

ME	AVERY
The woman.	A white girl walks in
She is braiding my hair	and asks for box braids
I ask her her name	*"On your own hair?"*
Aisa	*"Yeah. How much?"*
Aisha	
One of them.	And just like that no more talking/
	shop quiet
She may have said both.	No more:
One to me	Dot-dot-dot! (dot!)
And one to someone on the phone	Harlem/colony.
Calling to see if she can get her	
weave fixed	But then,
	I remember,
	Her braids will be fuzzy by Sunday.

She is
Putting my kinks—
Wrapping them in long blonde
ropes (long blonde ropes)
She's on the side
And a girl
A tiny girl from Senegal
Is on the back
Working through my kinks with a
Dollar store comb

Ripping

Ripping
Young girl ripping
Senegal, Senegal, I hear.
I smile.
I wish I could do more
For the young girl
Braiding my hair while
She waits to start school
Hopefully in two weeks, Aisha
says.
(Aisa)
Everybody's worried about their
Edges
                    (Edges)
                              (Edges)
          (Edges)

Everybody on they edges.

SMILING TUXEDOED MAN
Please don't snatch my edges

ME
Leave my edges

SMILING TUXEDOED MAN
Be careful with my edges.

A white girl walks in
and asks for box braids
"On your own hair?"
"Yeah. How much?"

And just like that no more talking
No more:
Dot-dot-dot! (dot!)
Harlem/colony.

But then,
I remember,
Her braids will be fuzzy by Sunday.

A white girl walks in
and asks for box braids
"On your own hair?"
"Yeah. How much?"

And just like that no more talking
No more:
Dot-dot-dot! (dot!)
Harlem/colony.

But then,
I remember,
Her braids will be fuzzy by Sunday.

A white girl walks in
and asks for box braids
"On your own hair?"
"Yeah. How much?"

ME
Everyone has concerns about edges
Four women
Four women
(Four women)
On my hair
Two
Then three
(Three)
I worry more for my ends.

SMILING TUXEDOED MAN
The ends are the elders
edges are where it begins
(where it all begins)

The young girl won't speak
Won't tell me her name
I wonder what she worries of:

Her ends in Senegal
Or her beginnings, here
Or maybe whatever is playing in
her headphones
While she darts dark eyes
around her steady fingers
And Aisha
(Aиsa)
Pays her son's college tuition

And just like that no more talking

No more:
Dot-dot-dot! (dot!)

Harlem/colony.
But then,
I remember,
Her braids will be fuzzy by Sunday.

A white girl walks in
and asks for box braids
"On your own hair?"
"Yeah. How much?"

And just like that no more talking
No more:
Dot-dot-dot! (dot!)

Harlem/colony.
But then,
I remember,
Her braids will be fuzzy by Sunday.

AVERY
Colony.
Cah. Lony.
Colony too muddied up too far in the
Distance
My colonizers sound—*Sounded*
I'm sure
The way I do now.
Which makes me less exotic to them
Than other blacks they haven't yet personally ruined.

Blacks from other places who can (and frankly should)
Weave in and out of their commitment to their blackhood.

There are a bunch of us living here
That don't have a choice.
Don't get to weave.
Our home is
Well this is it
There is no other place
Unless we divide ourselves into parts and spread ourselves across the
Western Coast of Africa

                                         ME
                                         Central

                                         SMILING TUXEDOED MAN
                                         Southeastern

To go back "home"
This
This is the place.
There is no There to go back to
If we wanted to
But somehow the picture of "patriot" is
Not ours.

{ALL}
YOU look over your shoulder

SMILING TUXEDOED MAN
Hoping no one is peeking at you
Through their curtains
Wondering who you are
And what you are doing
With your nose an inch from the
Muddied-up water of your color

A frog jumps
Reminding YOU to get out of dodge, too.

YOU get out of dodge.

It's a curious thing to feel out of place
Returning to the lip of the pond
You lost Your jump rope in
That time you and your sister went
"Fishing"
It's a strange thing to feel

Out of place
To feel
How did I?
How did we?
What was that?

In your own backyard
On the ground broken for you
For Your future.
YOU look over your shoulder
Hoping no one is peeking at you
Through their curtains
Wondering who you are
And what you are doing
With your nose an inch from the
Muddied-up water of your color

Suburbs were built for white people
To escape
The carnage they left behind when they refused to live next to niggers
YOU don't know any niggers
Except for the ones that poverty made
That hopelessness
That liquor made
That asbestos and broken science beekers
That crack
The FBI
That the systematic destruction of black leadership made
That rage made
That grief

Grief

YOU don't know any niggers
Except for the voice that tells you
YOU don't belong anywhere
That YOU better keep moving
Searching
YOU better not stop there
Or there
YOU best be gettin on now
Not safe not safe
Here

Keep on moving don't stop no don't look back
Keep on moving don't stop no don't look back

> SMILING TUXEDOED MAN *twirling a barrette around his fingers:*

SMILING TUXEDOED MAN
Does everyone have a sippie?
Ready? And—1, 2, 3, 4!
> *What does my whiteness have to do with you doo, doo—*

AVERY
No. Boo, boo, no.

SMILING TUXEDOED MAN
No?

AVERY
No

> *Inhale into:*

{ALL}
YOU are in a vine, in the breathing, meshy mess of the vine water racing to give life, to make life worth the cost. YOU are tiny, small, so insignificant yet integral

ME
for if you move over in the smallest measure you change the fate of a branch, a bird, a flower, a funeral, a wedding.

SMILING TUXEDOED MAN
You change the color of the next dragonfly hatching thirty feet away from here.

{ALL}
Here,
Here.

MOVEMENT 5:

Falling Apart

> BAD BAND *plays reprise of list of weap-*
> *ons music.* YOU *hold on to the tree by*
> *its knuckles.*

AVERY
This is my auntie—Whitney Houston; these are my cousins—Dorothy, Lena,
Ella, Janet, Mariah; this is my great grandmother—Black Pegasus; this is my
great grandfather—Prince; and this is my great great grandfather—Elegba.

SMILING TUXEDOED MAN
YOU hear nothing

> *It all stops.*

ME
Then—the sound of water rushing in.

> BAD BAND *plays prelude to "The Ruler*
> *of All Things Real." They're so badass.*
> *Bom-bom-bommmmm!*
>
> ME + BAD BAND *play "The Ruler of All*
> *Things Real."*
>
> ME *in front of an opaque mirror as pic-*
> *tures of white family flash by, wavy like*
> *water and dissolving.*

ME
I am also white. The percentage
I'm not exactly sure
but that's for another show
Unpacking that would have us underground
Until we all suffocate
but owning whiteness is on my to-do list
As I'm sure it is on yours.

The last frontier isn't the ocean bottom or space
The last frontier is the mind
Where WE can do all kinds of things to
Ascend our pain
Or keep it all the exact same.

My great-great grandfather gets me, here. Here, he stands apart from every-one—presumably sisters, cousins, brothers, nephews—no one I know. But he stands. Was he pulled in to the frame? Did he insist on placing his body here, to say "I am here, was here too, don't let no one tell you different." Or, "I am here because I have to be here because this is how things go and if things didn't go they way they go, I would be somewhere else." Or, or, or.

By now my great-great grandmother, his black, commonlaw wife (not pictured), has already given birth to three black children (also not pictured?). By now his black children have black children, and their black children will bring more black children. In five years and a couple of seasons, my mother will be born.

Here he stands in—separation? Obligation? In happenstance? Here he stands on the edge of a shadow, the edge of the structure, the edge of the group. Looking at someone with a lens...

I look at YOU.

Here he stands in—separation? Obligation? In happenstance? Here he stands on the edge of a shadow, the edge of the structure, the edge of the group. Looking at someone with a lens...

I look at YOU.

ME

> *Why are you so elusive?*
> *Keepin me close*
> *Then making me go away*
> *What is it that makes you feel so damn special?*
>
> *What makes you think you can push me around?*
> *I don't how*
> *You think you have*
> *Control*
> *Control*
> *Over me*
>
> *What makes me so exclusive?*
> *What makes you think*
> *You can just stomp right through*
> *What makes you take up all the oxygen?*
>
> *I wish I knew so that I*
> *Could do the same*
> *I wish I knew so that I*
> *Had*
> *Whatever it is you're smokin*
> *Whatever it is you're drinkin*
> *Whatever it is that has you thinkin*

You rule the world
You rule the world

SMILING TUXEDOED MAN *clears his throat.*
He reads from sheets of jumbo end papers.

SMILING TUXEDOED MAN + AVERY
An alternative list of weapons:

So, you're just black…That's it?
Is that your real hair?
No, but where are you *from?*
Can I touch it?
You know, I don't even think of you as black…
Hey…*Girl*friend!
If I was black, I'd totally wanna look like you.
You look just like [insert any black person at all].
I'm so jealous. I totally want to be black. No, seriously.
I do!
C'mon girl, you know I didn't mean it. You know I'm
joking. You know, you know, you know, you *know.*

What makes you so aggressive
What makes you love
When you're just hanging out?

What makes you blend in out here?
I don't know how your sharpness
Blinds me out
Out
Ouuuuuut

What makes you think you own me?
I wish I knew that thing that makes you so
So
The ruler of all things real
The ruler of all things real
The ruler of all things reaaaaal
The ruler of all things real
The ruler of all things real

AVERY
The antidote for freedom is shame.

SMILING TUXEDOED MAN / NIXON
Shame—

AVERY
Yes, Dick, it is.

They stare at each other.

SMILING TUXEDOED MAN / NIXON
I feel shame.

AVERY
Yes, Dick.

I used to have dreams that I'd float right round the Mississippi up and out of the river into the ocean and not know where I was goin but so excited to be goin. And I'd get up around get caught in a current or two somewhere around the foot of a sand dune in the distance. But I would stay calm cause I knew that I was bein carried somewhere important.

I always woke up before I got there. So I drink to help me sleep so's I can figure it out.

They stare at each other.

ME
Whiteness makes friends with itself
to build a fortress
around itself

It keeps itself from falling too far
by making the decision
To be less human—
Less forgiving,
Feeling
Less willing to be undone.
Whiteness is in the way of itself
And will always be
As long as the Heart of Whiteness
Is its invention of separateness

As long as it insists on keeping to itself

Despite the impossibility of the action.

Whiteness is my friend

Because I can look it in the eye
And see that it is nothing
Real.

So it is not a threat
No, not a threat,
though it howls from its spray-painted
Throne that thinks that it is gold.

Whiteness is not gold.
Whiteness is no-thing
but confused
and reaching out for
the Companionship of its own undoing
:

:

SMILING TUXEDOED MAN
White people don't move over on the sidewalk.
The vestiges of Jim Crow?
Maybe when the Irish were Irish or
Russians were Russians
Poles Poles
They made room
For the real whites
But now they all
Just band together
Clotheslining my Spirit, walking right through me
To get home and feed their pugs.
It would kill YOU to move—apparently.
White is
White means what?
For me to answer, or for you?

AVERY
"White" is the origin of you looking for me to find the conclusion.

SMILING TUXEDOED MAN
Boppity bop-bop. Bop!

> ME *begins the eh, eh chant.* AVERY *sings*
> *"Whatchu Lookin At?" while* ME *and*
> SMILING TUXEDOED MAN *back her.*

NIXON

Ladieees and laddies, Daddies and babies, awkward and tall, she's black—oops!—*back* for more spectacularity she's a rare-ity and if you can sparrrre … itty your eyes from your third glass of Happy, please welcome our unending Source of the Force back into the center of the light—Averyyyyyyyy Nolastnaaaaaaaaaaame!

AVERY

> *Whatchu lookin at*
> *Whatchu lookin through*
>
> *People talkin but*
> *Nothin's comin through*
> *And all I'm hearin is confusin*
> *And it makes me blue*
>
> *Nothing's making sense*
> *None of it is true*
>
> *And so I go*
> *Eh eh eh eh eh eh*
> *And so I go*
> *Eh eh eh eh eh eh*
> *And so I go*
> *Eh eh eh eh eh eh*
> *And so I go—*

ME

And this is my grandmother: Alyse Mildred Walker.

```
I
When I was six years old
My grandmother tried to get me back
She took us
took
this lady to court to try to get me back you know
To their family
But
The judge asked me
Where did I want to live
And I just tol em I wanted to live wit my foster mother
Cuz I had been with her all those years
You know
And but uhhh
```

Mother would come around some time
But you know
I
I didn't like her
It's a shame to say
I didn't like her then
Like I say
After I got grown
Actually before I got grown
Cuz this lady that raised me
Was movin down to Mississippi
And I didn't wanna go down theh
Cuz I had heard so many negative things about it
You know
And I
I just didn't see myself livin down there
So
When I was fourteen
I went to live wit my real mother
But see
I wudn't there long
I was only with her for two years
then I got married
So
Yep
Everybody say we look just alike I don't know
Hmm-hmm
But I never did know my
My
my father
whoever
You know
It's a shame to say
Whoever he was
But
I never did know my father.

{ALL}

Hot fire always on
Ready to burn up the place
Never gonna damp me out

I will combust through your walls

And make a case for the cause
Did I tell you to let go of me?

I am kerosene
Don't come for me

I am kerosene
Don't come for me

Burn like gasoline
Don't come for me
Don't come for me
Don't come for me

I am kerosene
Don't come for me

I am kerosene
Don't come for me

Burn like gasoline
Don't come for me
Don't come for me
Don't come for me

Hot fire can't be wrong
When the place goes up in flames
Never gonna turn it around
No-oh-oh-oh-oh-oh-oh

Ash can't be made undone
The way the war is won
Destroys our resolution

I am kerosene
Don't come for me

I am kerosene
Don't come for me

Burn like gasoline
Don't come for me
Don't come for me
Don't come for me

I am kerosene
Don't come for me

I am kerosene
Don't come for me

Burn like gasoline
Don't come for me
Don't come for me
Don't come for me

I am
kerosene

I am kerosene!

Jerrican
Jerrican
Jerrican
Jerrican
Burn me down to wax

Jerrican
Jerrican
Jerrican
Jerrican
Burn me down to wax

Jerrican
Jerrican
Jerrican
Jerrican
Take my plastic
And make it tan

Jerrican
Jerrican
Jerrican
Jerrican
Burn me down to wax

MOVEMENT 6:

Reclamation

ME
I see the house
I want to get close to the house
But I'm afraid of snakes and things
Catchin on me
And I'm in my twenties
But I'm afraid to ask
Too many questions
The wrong questions

In my grandmother's house
There are white Jesuses everywhere
Like there are in many black grandmothers' houses
Kitchen bathroom
Living room

White prayer hands in the back room
We replaced the white cherubic children
On the wall with my great grandfather
And a photo of a cousin,
the one who paid my grandfather's fraternity dues
none of us ever met
We replaced them two years ago
Finally
After I asked who the white cherubic children were on the wall
Who watched over me while I slept
As I've grown older
I think they do not look
I think they stare
I think they want to eat my skin
And swallow my hair
And make me slick and clean and
They do not like me
They do not want
Me
They want cleanliness
And peace
And the older I grow
The more I am not peaceful
The more white Cherubims
And prayer hands become charred in my mind
And I only want to scream about the lost murders
And solve the puzzles
And take the picture frames off of the wall.

This cousin
The one none of us ever met
He fought in WWII we think
My grandfather showed me his burial flag.
It was in the closet. Still folded—
Tucked behind my grandfather's sweaters.

The sound of water.
An American flag.

ME
I look at YOU.
YOU see.

Beat.

ME
This is my great-grandfather:

And this is my—

Name Unknown

Whom I call
"Henrietta."

Birth
Unknown

Death
Unknown
Dash—

Henrietta,

What was your favorite color?
How did you endure?

What was your favorite color?
How did you endure?

Henrietta, I am yours.
You, mine.

Henrietta, where there are holes
Can we patch Wholeness together
To make something new?

Where there are holes,

can wholeness come through,
Rushing in to greet us where we least expect
Meeting.

I am yours and you are mine.

And here We are
together.

SMILING TUXEDOED MAN
Would you like to see my family?

YOU see a slide of Lignin:

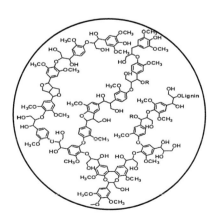

Sometime during this speech, the word "Ascension" appears on the projector screen.

SMILING TUXEDOED MAN

Lignin made trees possible. Now, Life could build upward, and this opened a whole new territory. A three-dimensional matrix for communities far above the ground. Earth became the planet of the trees. But Lignin had a downside: it was hard to swallow.

ME
It took the fungi and bacteria millions of years to evolve the biochemical means to consume it. In the meantime, the trees just kept springing up, falling, dying over and getting buried by the mud that built up over eons. Eventually there were hundreds of billions of trees entombed in the Earth, buried forests all over the earth.

ME
I look at YOU.
YOU look.

Beat.

My last name is Walker
I'm destined to take the next right step
I guess
No
I sure am
Destined to take the next right step
I've never really thought much of my name
I'm not a boy
So
That makes sense
Boys are taught to think
You know
About their progeny
The seed!
Plant the seed!
The sound they carry in their—
WALKER
WALK
Er
But lately I've just needed the step
To step through the grief
To pass through the
Not thinking I'm okay somehow,
when I'm clearly okay
More than okay
Step step
Until my foot
Opens up my left lung
And the breath comes up and out

And I make sound
I've been wanting to visit the Walker Plantation
It's in Arkansas—
is?
Was.
But I've been wondering off the plantations I've got
Runnin around in fields of my story
What that one was like.
What Master WALKER was like
WALKER.
Was he slow?
Did he do everything slowed down
Make his money slow
Steady
Just the next barrel
Then the next
Did he build his wealth like molasses?
Or, was he one of those masters that like,
Didn't even really make a lot because
Even though he owned people
and ran people
He didn't know how to turn a profit
And he died destitute and dumb
and absent of riches
to carry forward to his offspring?
The Walkers
mine
really don't rush.
Used to drive me a little crazy when
I was little and visiting
Cuz it wasn't much to do
Just sit
Listen to the screen door slam
Double
Double
Watch flies collect on the fly paper
The tractor didn't even work.
By the time I was on the scene
It was already rusted.
But one day
I swear this

One day, my grandaddy walked by me
Real slow
Like he did
The way retired security guards do
He sat down
And he said he wanted to show me something
His eyes lit from inside
More than anything in the garage with a plug
And as I looked
The way magical granddaughters look
He sat the stillest
Most patient I've seen a human sit
And then the something
He caught a fly straight outta the air
With his giant hands
And then he looked at me
And he grinned
And I got to see his gold tooth
And he got to see my pink tongue
As my mouth shot open in an awe
That only happens
When you haven't yet been told
By the world that girls like you
Should never believe in magic
SO
I've always held that
Fly
And carried it around
Underneath my name
And it's just been growin
And growin bigger than the memory
Of some master
Who's palace has long since crumbled
And is probably now an autozone
Or a wal-mart
And I've been thinking
That Walker is a brilliant name for me
Because I seem to get the
Next right step
In magical, magical ways.

ME + BAD BAND *transitions to "While the Sun Waits for You."*

ME

> *While the sun waits for you*
> *Bless his honor*
> *Bless his honor*
> *While the sun waits for you*
> *Bless his honor*
> *Bless his honor*

{ALL}

> *While the moon waits for you*
> *Bless her honor*
> *Bless her honor*
> *While the moon waits for you*
> *Bless her honor*
> *Bless her honor*
> *Ahhhh*
> *Ahhhhhh*
> *Ahhhhhhhh*
> *Ahhhhh*

AVERY

No. *(Microbeat)* You know, you know that moment when you re-enter the house after you've been out on the porch in the high sunshine and your eyes haven't re-adjusted? You open the screen door and you go back in the house. You hear that unique slam: CLACK!, you know, and for a moment, it's so dark in there! So dark. But I like that moment because it makes me stand still and feel my feet again and op! I'm back on the carpet, yes for sure the carpet and not the porch. I'm back from the World, and when my eyes adjust I can find somewhere to set down and rest.

Beat.

If I had a nickel for every time I heard somebody say somethin about the dark. So negative. But dark makes you wait. You just have to take your time in it and stop actin like you know everything, even if it's only dark for a moment. For a moment you know nothing. You have no context. Until—you listen. Listen and open your body to new kinds of feelin that just don't happen until you come in from the porch and shut that door. Sun gives us all the information.
Dark needs our faith.

ME
I say to YOU:
I realize that when a grandmother says
I am proud of you
to a granddaughter
what she is saying is
I am filled from the inside
Filled with joy
To see you breaking through
YOU are breaking through
Farther than I got
Than I could get
you are pushing a wall
That was built around the bottom of my trunk
My roots cracked it some
And you are breaking through
What she is really saying is
Thank God for you
Thank God for your plane ticket
Thank God it was worth everything
That broke my branches
Thank God your eyes
Remain white and open and unblinded
I am proud of US
Proud of US
Proud of what I birthed
That birthed you
And you can do what you like about that
You can do what you like because
I did enough
I did just enough
To make you
Exist
And *you* exist.
And she is saying
I see
I see

{ALL}
{I see} {I see} {I see}

ME
And she is proud the ground is solid
Because she made it So.

> *The sound of barrettes clinking.*

While the sun waits for you
Bless his honor
Bless his honor
While the stars wait for you
Bless their honor
Bless their honor
While the moon waits for you
Bless her honor
Bless her honor

> ME *and* YOU *breathe.*

End of Play.

AFTERWORD

I am right now, as I'm writing these words, at home. But here isn't the home where I can typically be found in New York. Rather I'm at my ancestral domain that rivers and shoals the midlands of Tennessee. Though here today, many of my folks migrated from further north of here, homegrown in the Midwest states, very near to the sound, shoals, and souls who Jillian Walker's work celebrates. Work is a very important word to people like us who come from those who had forced or limited choice in the matter and manner of their work. Celebration, too, to us, is a vital necessity. These words, like Jillian's, are the work of celebration and story. No mere matter. Not simply a narrative in the manner of place. These words, like us, are much, much more.

Jillian Walker is a deep river. Said another way, the simpler modes of storytelling & seeing the world—which is to say, the determinations of settler colonial imaginations—cannot contain her. This is among the powers of SKiNFoLK, as well as the unfettered realms of wonder which embody the body of works that are Jillian Walker. Let's call it: The Walker work. Indeed, it's unconcerned with the fetishes and fixations most artists willingly apply to market to audiences who live in fear of misunderstanding rituals which they were never meant to know at all. O, yes! The Walker work is not about you; rather it abides around and amongst. These worlds must be witnessed by feeling. Her plays demand our intimacy, our attention while they breathe in sorrow and exhale praise. The pleasure they seek to offer need not be reciprocated. Why? Because Walker work is a reservoir of glorious conviction. Its water is steady, flowing freely from within. And while you're welcome to drink these gifts, frankly, neither presence nor applause are the aim of her offerings. Walker work will work—whether you like it or not. Like all good medicines, its power is one part mystery, one part its hopefulness to heal.

In an art world suffering from subterfuge and virtue signaling, the Walker work is for real. Her stories have to have been lived in, which is why we too must live within them. Her dead are made reborn, right before our eyes, by way of love. This is no easy feat. No artificial intelligence. What Jillian Walker writes could not be made by manufacture or machine. Black wisdom is divine wisdom. These are spiritual technologies, sourced from a pantheon rooted deep within the inner river. Inside workings; embodied bodies. Of course, I've failed to mention the playful intellect and anthropological intensity of the Walker work. For once might we dispense with tired academic-ese such as interdisciplinary and mixed media? It's time we abolish the ways in which so much Black art, when written about, is repudiated, or worse, reduced. I for one refuse to be made reductive.

Jillian Walker is fierce, unapologetic, and fulsome. Also, Jillian Walker is her work. Therefore, the work and worker are one in the same: a fusion of mutual ferocity. The story is the skin and vice versa.

No one was ever born in a theater. And yet, for many, the theater is a place we go to encounter notions of home. Notions of kinship, questions of care, notes towards love. These are longings that clamor deep within our bones. To reach us there, Jillian Walker crafts a venerable melody to moisturize, to permeate us beyond the skin. Her reverberation has remained with me and will with you, resounding and comforting your spirit. Won't you celebrate with me the rare work she has gathered us here to hear.

– Phillip Howze, August 2023

SCORES

by Jillian Walker
& Kasaun Henry

WE GO DOWN

Churchy-Funky

Jillian Walker
Kasaun Henry

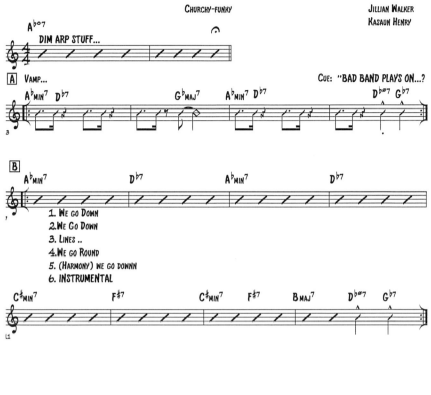

1. We Go Down
2. We Go Down
3. Lines ..
4. We go Round
5. (Harmony) we go downn
6. Instrumental

WHAT DOES MY BLACKNESS HAVE TO DO WITH YOU

NEO-SOUL-ISH

JILLIAN WALKER
KASAUN HENRY

3x

A MIN   G   A MIN   G

1. INTRO
2. I AM THE GREATEST... MYTH
3. AND YOU SPEAK MY....

A A MIN   G   A MIN   G

5   VOX: I WAS AROUND BEFORE PLATO. I WAS ALIVE BEFORE TIME....

F   E MIN   D

9

B VOX+ PNO LH

13 WHAT DOES MY BLACK-NESS   HAVE TO DO WITH YOU   BOO BOO   BOO BOO BOO BOO   BOO ___ BOO BOO BOO

17 WHAT DOES MY BLACK-NESS   HAVE TO DO WITH YOU   BOO BOO   BOO BOO BOO BOO   BOO ___ BOO

I CAN'T DO IT ANYMORE

AFRICAN AMERICAN

Jillian Walker
Kasaun Henry

THIS IS A CALL TO MY NEXT OF KIN

Jillian Walker
Kasaun Henry

PORTAL

Jillian Walker
Kasaun Henry

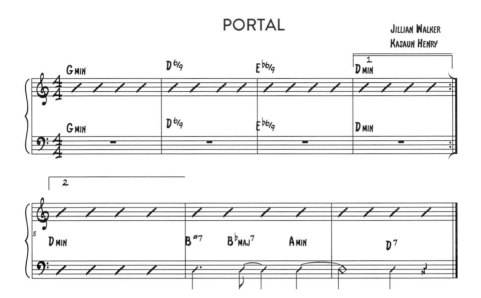

SOME OF YOU ARE DRUNK

Jillian Walker
Kasaun Henry

Some of you are drunk and you hear Ang-els   Some of you are drunk and you hear Ang-els

Some of you are drunk and you hear Ang-els

Some   of   you   are   Drunk   and   you   hear   Ang - els

RULER

CUE: "I LOOK AT YOU....."

JILLIAN WALKER
KASAUN HENRY

KEROSENE

JILLIAN WALKER
KASAUN HENRY

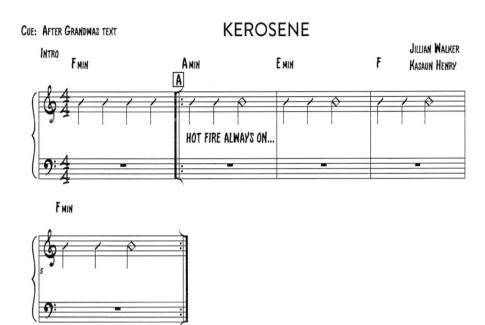

HOT FIRE ALWAYS ON...

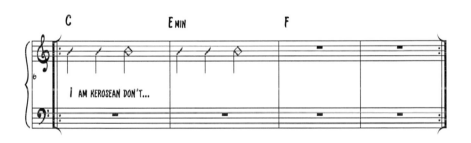

I AM KEROSEAN DON'T...

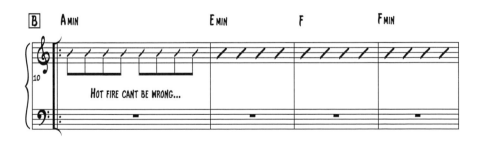

HOT FIRE CANT BE WRONG...

JERRICAN

Jillian Walker
Kasaun Henry

WHILE THE SUN WAITS

JILLIAN WALKER
KASAUN HENRY

CONTRIBUTORS

Jillian Walker :: Gogo Yema is a multidimensional artist (composer, playwright, performer, vocalist, dramaturg), diviner, healer, teacher, and Sangoma Priestess. She is a guide of Ancestral healing, spirituality and creative consciousness through multiple dimensions, back and forward generationally across timelines, bloodlines, and legacy.

With her spiritual practice as the central portal, she has created and supported over a decade of art in the fields of theater and performance, music, film, television, as well as throughout the academy, in healing spaces, women's circles, prisons, places of worship, and sacred spaces at and across the oceans.

She blesses the honor of her lineages through performance and practice. Her most acclaimed work, *SKiNFoLK: An American Show* (The Bushwick Starr/National Black Theatre: NY Times Critics Pick, Kilroys List, Lilly Award) is published by 53rd State Press. Her other plays and projects have received numerous honors and include *Songs of Speculation* (JACK, 2020 Third Coast Audio Unbound Award) and *Sarah's Salt.*(Winner Columbia@ Roundabout, Bay Area Playwrights Festival Finalist, Relentless Award honorable mention). Her latest onstage script(ure), *The Whitney Album*, appeared in Soho Rep's '22-'23 season.

One of Gogo's favorite descriptions of her onstage work comes from Poet and Prophet Alexis Pauline Gumbs, who described her Joe's Pub concert, *Blue Ink*, as "Transformational, Black feminist, ancestral-portal-opening, love-centered musical work."

With her multifaceted training and education in traditional academic spaces (BA: The University of Michigan, MFA: Columbia University) and ancient afro-indigenous traditions (Chief teachers, Makhosi Himi Gogo Thule Ngane, Queen Baba Solstice Kha Ekhaya Esima, Makhosi Foundation), Jillian :: Gogo holds a unique combination of intellectual curiosity, spiritual rigor and an incredible capacity for deep listening and collaboration with people, built and natural worlds, time/space, Ancestors and all of the unseen.

Some of Gogo's favorite collaborations include: writing/performing and serving as Process Director with The TEAM (*Reconstructing*), creating Move, Meditate, Make with Libby King, holding prompt-based performance classes with the students at The University of Washington and Harvard, holding circle with the women in Nisha Moodley's Soul of Leadership, and sitting in prayer, song and healing space with her spiritual family at the Makhosi Foundation.

BLK GRK (or, hiding in plain sight), a multiversal, poetic film exploration of the history of Black Greek Letter Organizations, is a deep upcoming collaboration with co-conceivers, Rachel Chavkin and Eric Berryman, and has expanded Jillian into its screenwriter, composer and star, alongside Eric Berryman.

Gogo is also deepening in collaboration with fellow artists, culture-shifters and devoted leaders as the Founding Artist and Studio Mother of her own sacred healing house, *Legasea*, opening its doors in the Fall of 2023.

From a heartspace that flows out of The Love of the Ancestors, she continues to incite and inspire sublime new forms of art, structures, and communal systems that break the brutal boundaries of the colonial imagination.

Dr. Kasaun Henry is a public intellectual, motivational speaker, award-winning filmmaker, composer, music theorist, and international music producer from Harlem, New York. His rich history as an intellectual, an artist, and a philosopher are deeply influenced by his upbringing in Harlem. He was the captain of the historic chess team the Raging Rooks and led two national championship teams in 1991 and 1998.

Kasaun is a dedicated educator, writer, philosopher and lecturer of social thought and an advocate for enlightened humanity. He uses his experiences and vast knowledge base to inspire possibilities and provide motivation in his community and the general public. He has taught and given lectures at private and public schools of all age levels, community and renowned colleges (Hudson County Community College, The University of Michigan, Bloomfield College), corporations, churches, and community centers. His wide-ranging interests as a speaker cover areas such as education, history, philosophy, religion and music. Kasaun hosts the "PoliticalSoulFood Podcast" on which he discusses politics, education and history in an accessible and passionate conversation for the youth and the general public. He also transformed his PoliticalSoulFood work into a film series that captures the issues and realities of Black life in Harlem through his production company, Harlemwood Studios.

Kasaun holds a Ph.D. in History & Culture from Drew University, a Master's in History and Culture (Drew University), Master of Letters, concentration in Philosophy (Faulkner University) and a Master's in Music Theory (University of Michigan). Presently, his academic interests are Black intellectual history, history of human rights, and theories of secularization.

Phillip Howze is an American playwright and educator whose works have been produced at theaters across the country. He's a 2021 Jerome Hill Artist Fellow, a MAP Fund recipient, and a Resident Writer at Lincoln Center Theater/LCT3 where he's also commissioned to write a new play. Recently he was appointed the Associate Senior Lecturer at Harvard University's Theater, Dance & Media program. His writing has been published by *American Theatre* magazine and 53rd State Press, and his new play collection *Rarities & Wonders: Plays* is available from Tripwire Harlot Press.

Nia O. Witherspoon is a Black queer multidisciplinary artist + healing justice practitioner investigating the metaphysics of black liberation, desire, and diaspora, as they track across the space-time continuum. Combining Black feminism, indigenous epistemologies, eco-feminism, and auto-critogrophy with mediums in writing, performance, sound, and installation, Witherspoon creates portals for communion, witnessing, and healing. Current and recent works include: *Priestess of Twerk: A Black Femme Temple* (HERE Art Center/Musical Theatre Factory, 2024), *Chronicle X: The Dark Girl Chronicles* (The Shed, 2021), and *MESSIAH* (La Mama, 2019). She is a NEFA/NTP recipient, a Creative Capital Awardee, a Jerome New Artist Fellow, a current artist in residence at HERE Art Center and Musical Theatre Factory, and former resident at BAX/Brooklyn Arts Exchange and

New York Theatre Workshop. Her work has been or will be featured by The Shed, BRIC, Oregon Shakespeare Festival, Joe's Pub, HERE, JACK, La Mama ETC, Playwright's Realm, Links Hall, National Black Theatre, Brava Theatre, BAAD, Movement Research, BAX, Dixon Place, Painted Bride, 651 Arts, and elsewhere. Her writing is published in the *Journal of Popular Culture*; *Imagined Theatres*; *Women and Collective Creation*; and *IMANIMAN: Poets Writing in the Anzaldúan Borderlands*. She holds a BA in American Studies from Smith College, a PhD from Stanford University in Theatre and Performance Studies, and has held academic appointments at Florida State University, Arizona State University, University of Massachusetts, Fordham University, and BerkleeNYC.

ACKNOWLEDGMENTS

Deep gratitude to all who've supported the genesis of *SKiNFOLK*, living and ascended. Some names of people, places, points in time that this work formed in while I listened: The Performance Art class at Columbia University School of the Arts, Morgan Jenness, Ethics of Aesthetics, and SOA Dramaturgy class of 2017. Christian Parker and Leslie Ayvazian. Daaimah Mubashshir, William Burke, John del Gaudio and the Starr Reading Series. Noel Allain, Sue Kessler, Lauren Miller, Jehan O. Young, and The Bushwick Starr. Awoye Timpo. Ars Nova. 104th Street. 145th Street. 151st. Catwalk and Catstkill, NY. Mei Ann Teo. Ned Moore, Olivia O'connor, and Pittsburgh CLO's Spark Festival. That hotel and the bathrobes that Mei Ann and I wore while we put the script on the floor and listened. Kasaun Eric Henry. All of you. Bryce Collins. Jason Smith. Jonathan McCrory. Sade Lythcott. The whole creative team of the Bushwick Starr/National Black Theater production (please look up everyone's names, dear reader). All of the creative teams before that one. Please look up the names.

Dad. Mom. Jasmine. Mama Nita. Papa. Kennedy. Morgan. Diggy. Danielle, Rachel. Uncle Rick. Auntie. Joe. The neighbors on Adrian who gave money and made sure it got to the Starr. The Sorors. The Boule brothers. Three Brothers Theatre in Waukegan, IL.

All of the people who came to every iteration that has lived so far.

The people who crashed opening night in Brooklyn to dance with us because my family is that irresistible.

Kate Kremer. Eisa Davis. Nia. Philip...

These are some. There are many more. All of the names on the family tree poster my father printed while we raised money to make the first show appear out of thin air. I still have your signatures. Some of you have died since then. This work is part of the candle that will never go out as long as there are libraries. And then whatever comes after the libraries. There are many more names I am still learning. The Ancestors who continue to bring me home. Thank you for loving me with a love so fierce I only know how to sing it.

What you, all of you, have woven into this work lives embedded in its heart, and in Mine. I thank you for it all.

-JW

ABOUT THE PRESS

53rd State Press publishes lucid, challenging, and lively new writing for performance. Our catalog includes new plays as well as scores and notations for interdisciplinary performance, graphic adaptations, and essays on theater and dance.

53rd State Press was founded in 2007 by Karinne Keithley in response to the bounty of new writing in the downtown New York community that was not available except in the occasional reading or short-lived performance. In 2010, Antje Oegel joined her as a co-editor. In 2017, Kate Kremer took on the leadership of the volunteer editorial collective. For more information or to order books, please visit 53rdstatepress.org.

53rd State Press books are represented to the trade by TCG (Theatre Communications Group). TCG books are exclusively distributed to the book trade by Consortium Book Sales and Distribution, an Ingram Brand.

LAND & LABOR ACKNOWLEDGMENTS

53rd State Press recognizes that much of the work we publish was first developed and performed on the unceded lands of the Lenape and Canarsie communities. Our books are stored on and shipped from the unceded lands of the Chickasaw, Cherokee, Shawnee, and Yuchi communities. The work that we do draws on natural resources that members of the Indigenous Diaspora have led the way in protecting and caretaking. We are grateful to these Indigenous communities, and commit to supporting Indigenous-led movements working to undo the harms of colonization.

As a press devoted to preserving the ephemeral experiments of the contemporary avant-garde, we recognize with great reverence the work of radical BIPOC artists whose (often uncompensated) experiments have been subject to erasure, appropriation, marginalization, and theft. We commit to amplifying the revolutionary experiments of earlier generations of BIPOC theatermakers, and to publishing, promoting, celebrating, and compensating the BIPOC playwrights and performers revolutionizing the field today.

SKinFoLK: An American Show is made possible by the New York State Council on the Arts with the support of the Office of the Governor and the New York State Legislature.

53rd State Press
new writing for performance